July 16, 1976

A Adela —

　　A people great —

　　　A people Old —

Inside this book

　　Our story is told.

　　　　　Neshama Ami

They All Are Jews

BIOGRAPHICAL SKETCHES

BY

MAC DAVIS

WITH

PORTRAITS BY

E. E. CLARIDGE

From Moses to Einstein

THEY
ALL
ARE
JEWS

REVISED EDITION

JORDAN PUBLISHING CO., NEW YORK

They You Are About to Meet

5

NATHAN STRAUSS . . . . *Prince of the Generous Heart*

OTTO LILIENTHAL . . . . *The Bird Man*

ALBERT MICHELSON . . . . *He Measured the Speed of Light*

EHRLICH AND WASSERMANN . . *Heroes of the Laboratory*

LOUIS BRANDEIS . . . . *Friend of Justice and of Man*

SIGMUND FREUD . . . . *Explorer of the Human Mind*

ADOLPH OCHS . . . . *All the News That's Fit to Print*

ALFRED DREYFUS . . . . *Devil's Island Could Not Crush His Spirit*

RUFUS DANIEL ISAACS . . . . . . *Viceroy of India*

THEODORE HERZL . . . . *"If I Forget Thee, O Jerusalem"*

ARTHUR SCHNITZLER . . . . *Master of Twilight Moods*

ISRAEL ZANGWILL . . . . *The Jewish Dickens*

CARL LAEMMLE . . . . *Little Giant*

LILLIAN WALD . . . . *The Angel of Henry Street*

KARL LANDSTEINER . . . . *The Blood Detective*

BERNARD MANNES BARUCH . . . *Intimate of Presidents*

SIR HERBERT SAMUEL . . . . *First High Commissioner of Palestine*

CHAIM WEIZMANN . . . . *Builder of the Jewish Homeland*

MAX REINHARDT . . . . *"All the World's a Stage"*

STEPHEN SAMUEL WISE . . . . . . *The Voice for Human Rights*

HERBERT H. LEHMAN . . . . *Chief of the Empire State*

LEON BLUM . . . . *France's Master of Destiny*

LEON TROTSKY . . . . *Forsaken Napoleon*

JACOB EPSTEIN . . . . *Storm Center of Sculpture*

CASIMIR FUNK . . . . *Isolator of the Vitamin*

DAVID SARNOFF . . . . *S O S*

GEORGE GERSHWIN . . . . *From Tin Pan Alley to Carnegie Hall*

JASHA HEIFETZ . . . . *Knight of the Bow*

ALBERT EINSTEIN . . . . *Map-Maker of a Universe*

Introduction

YOU are about to meet sixty Jewish men and women: soldier, statesman, explorer, scholar, pugilist, poet, scientist, rabbi, actress, business man. The highlights in the extraordinary lives of these heroes and heroines are briefly told. Rogue or prophet, satan or savior, I have placed no halo about their heads. Perhaps they are not the greatest one might have chosen, but their deeds are so immense and so varied in scope, that as a group they compose practically the history and progress of the Jew through civilization.

It is interesting to conjecture what might have happened to many dwelling within the covers of this book if Fate had played her hand differently. If a gruff Prussian sergeant, a gatekeeper at the Berlin border, had remained stubborn and refused to admit to the German capital a stuttering, hunchback Yeshiva boy, would the world have come to know of Moses Mendelssohn? If a pious, old, scholarly Jew had insisted that his five sons remain in their Ghetto home and become scholars instead of sending them off to foreign lands to be tradesmen, would the House of Rothschild have written the most spectacular chapter in the financial and political history of Europe? If Spinoza had not been cursed by his own people and driven from his home, would he have become the greatest philosopher of modern times? If his mother had not bought a second-hand piano, would George Gershwin have come to write the songs of a nation? All these are melodramatic ifs that shaped not only great careers, but also, in many instances, the history of the world.

Biography has its purpose; there is some pleasure in it. To the youth these stories will reveal the possibilities to which Jews may aspire, while to the grown-up they will help give companionship with the great. They may even arouse in us a wistful feeling that we too might have grasped the stars if Fate and circumstance had been a little kinder.

In this calendar of heroes and heroines, you will find melodrama, ambition, power, courage, love, despair, poverty, and all the influences that make greatness. So let us turn the pages and skip through time. Heroes and heroines! Here they are!

MAC DAVIS.

Moses
(——)
"LET MY PEOPLE GO"

Moses

FOR more than four hundred years the Israelites were slaves in Egypt. Rameses II, fearing that these slaves might grow far too numerous and powerful, commanded that all new-born male children of the Hebrews be killed. One woman, however, saved her son by hiding him in a cradle-ark by the river bank. And Pharaoh's daughter, coming down by the river, found the cradle, took the child to the palace, and adopted him as her son.

Moses was brought up luxuriously in the palace as an Egyptian prince. One day, grown to manhood, Moses wandered among the slave gangs and saw an overseer beating a Hebrew. His anger aroused, he killed the Egyptian. To escape the wrath of Pharaoh, he fled to the desert. In Median, he lived for years as a shepherd, restlessly dreaming of the day when he would free his people from slavery.

In the vast solitude of the desert, he became conscious of the divine presence of Jehovah. As he was tending his sheep, he saw a bush aflame with fire and yet it was not consumed. This was an omen to Moses that the time had come to free his people from bondage. He returned to Egypt, overcame the might and power of Pharaoh and led the Israelites to freedom and a new life.

For forty years they wandered through the desert. Moses faced revolt and mutiny, and the enemy's attacks, but drove his people relentlessly on to the Promised Land. Moses was their law-giver and taught them to love and worship God. He went atop Mount Sinai and forty days later he came down with two stone tablets upon which were inscribed the Ten Commandments, the foundation of the moral law of the civilized nations of the world.

Finally the Israelites came to the east bank of the Jordan. But Moses did not enter the Promised Land. He was old and weary. The voice of God had told him that a younger man must now take up his task. And as the people marched off to the Promised Land, Moses remained alone with his God. Legends say that Moses died the death of no common man. Legends also say that the moaning of the wind high up on the mountain of Nebo is the voice of Moses sighing in sorrow as he broods over the people he loved so well.

Bar Cochba

(–135 C.E.)
MAGNIFICENT WARRIOR

Bar Cochba

IN 117 c.e., with its independence lost and its Temple destroyed, Israel suffered under the oppression of the Roman yoke. Suddenly, in the midst of the humbled Jews, appeared Bar Cochba, calling them to arms. He was a warrior of tremendous bodily strength and flaming personality. Jewish soldiers from many regions flocked to his banners. Legends tell that to test the valor of a soldier, Bar Cochba would command him to cut off a finger at one stroke, or a horseman to tear up a Lebanon cedar by its roots while riding at full speed. Four hundred thousand soldiers enlisted under his command.

In the caves and hollow chalk mountains of Judea these insurgents secretly prepared for the day when they would rise and free Palestine from paganism. The Roman Emperor Hadrian ordered that Jerusalem be rebuilt as a pagan city, and the hatred of the Jews for the Romans burst into fury. Bar Cochba and his army marched forth against the Roman legions. For three years he waged a victorious war. Fifty strongholds and a thousand towns were captured. His military genius and extraordinary bravery terrified Hadrian, who massed all his legions in a desperate attempt to put down the rebellion. Bar Cochba made his last stand at the ancient city of Bethar. For a whole year he held back a Roman army three times the size of his own. But at last, in 135 c.e., his army fell, and the avenging Romans entered the city. For three days and three nights they massacred and pillaged. More than half a million Jews were slain, and thousands were sold into slavery.

No one knows how the mighty Bar Cochba met his death. A soldier brought his head to the Roman general and boasted that it was he who had slain him. But later Bar Cochba's body was found at the walls of the city, crushed by a snake. Thus passed the greatest of Jewish warriors, and so ended the last armed struggle of the Hebrew nation to win its independence.

Moses Maimonides

(1135–1204)

THE SECOND MOSES

Moses Maimonides

IN THE old Moorish city of Cordova, Spain, on a Passover eve during the Middle Ages, there was born one Moses ben Maimon, more generally known as Maimonides. Until his thirteenth year his life was peaceful. Then the fanatical Moors swept over from North Africa to kill and plunder all non-believers, and the Maimon family fled for its life. For twelve years, escaping death many times, they wandered over Spain until finally they settled in Cairo, Egypt. There Maimonides remained to the end of his days.

A young man of great wisdom, he followed in the path of his fathers and took up his duties as a rabbi, but to earn a livelihood he studied medicine. His fame as a surgeon spread and he was summoned to the royal court and made personal physician to the Sultan. He became famed as a Talmudist, philosopher, astronomer and physician. At fifty-two he completed his "Moreh"—The Guide for the Perplexed—which codified and made a clear and orderly construction of the Talmud. His other great work, which took him thirty years to complete, was the "Mishnah Torah," explaining the Jewish law and tradition from every source. From it came the well-known thirteen articles which to this day are repeated and sung in the synagogues.

From dawn to nightfall Maimonides labored to help the poor and helpless. His entire life was devoted to good works, and after eight centuries Jews still find in his memory a fresh courage, and in his teachings a troubled world finds a philosophy of truth and wisdom. His tomb stands at Tiberias in the Holy Land, and pilgrims from the four corners of the earth flock to this sacred shrine to pay their tribute to the memory of the great Maimonides.

Luis de Torres
(—)

HE SAILED WITH COLUMBUS

Luis de Torres

A LITTLE fleet of three sailing craft drifted in strange waters on October 12, 1492. On board was Christopher Columbus and his crew of one hundred and twenty men. Food was running low, the drinking water was almost gone; most of the men were muttering of mutiny, terrified at the recollection of the dreary months of ocean hazards, and more frightened of the unknown dangers that awaited them. They had left Spain months before to discover a new passage to India—maybe they would find the mythical land of gold. Suddenly a sailor at the lookout sighted a gleam of fire in the distance. Firing the bombard, he shouted, "Land ho!" It was the New World. Watching on the shore stood a strange, copper-colored race. From his flagship, Columbus summoned Luis de Torres, and sent him with one companion to parley with the Indians. De Torres went ashore—the first white man and European to set foot on the American continent. The half-naked men and women who spoke no tongue known to white men could not understand these strange travelers, but de Torres made himself understood by gestures, and soon the Indians welcomed Columbus and his men ashore.

Luis de Torres was a Marano Jew. These were the "damned" or secret Jews who, to escape persecution and death at the hands of the Inquisition, were converted to Christianity, but at heart remained Jews and secretly practiced their religion. Learned and fluent in many languages, de Torres was taken on the voyage to act as interpreter and sailed with Columbus the day after the expulsion of the Jews from Spain. So favorably impressed did he become with the new country, that when Columbus returned to Spain, de Torres remained in the New World. He was the first white man to discover tobacco and introduce its use into the Old World. In the new land, free from persecution, de Torres settled in what is now Cuba. There he remained, raising tobacco and trading with the Indians, who venerated him as the first white brother to come to their world from the unknown places beyond the sea.

Asser Levy
(–1680)
THE FIGHTING BUTCHER

Asser Levy

I N SEPTEMBER, 1654, there arrived in New York, then known as New Amsterdam, twenty-three penniless Jewish refugees. They had come after a perilous sea voyage to escape the tortures of the Portuguese Inquisition. Peter Stuyvesant, Dutch Governor of New Amsterdam, was hostile to the new settlers. He openly showed his prejudice by imposing numerous restrictions upon them. Asser Levy, one of the immigrants, opened a little meat shop, but he was ordered to keep his doors locked and thus could not trade. The other Jews were restricted in like manner.

Levy was a fighting man. Quickly he rallied the handful of frightened and discouraged Jews, and so forcibly argued his rights before Stuyvesant that the governor was compelled to rescind the unjust order. From then on, Levy became a champion for his people. When he discovered that a tax was to be levied upon Jews in lieu of military service, he fought and won the right for the Jew to serve and stand guard with the others as a soldier of New Amsterdam. Soon he gained full burgher rights and privileges for the Jewish settlers. He became a prominent trader and owner of a large slaughter house. Because he was honest, wise and trustworthy, many Christian merchants named Levy in their wills executor and custodian of their properties. He never betrayed a trust. He became the first Jewish landowner in New Amsterdam, and upon his land was built the first Jewish synagogue in North America. A patriot, he also contributed money towards the building of fortifications. When he died he was one of the wealthiest and most respected burghers of the New World. It was this fighting butcher who laid the foundation for racial and religious freedom that helped make New York City the home of the largest Jewish urban population in the world.

Baruch Spinoza

(1632–1677)

MARTYR TO TRUTH

Baruch Spinoza

A NIGHT in 1656. The synagogue in Amsterdam flickers with the light of many candles. Before the council of elders stands twenty-two-year-old Baruch Spinoza. He is accused of a grave charge—heresy. With faltering voice the old rabbi who had taught him as a boy says, "Retract and repent." But Spinoza is silent. And the rabbi begins to read the *Cherem*, the ban of excommunication. "Hereafter no one shall speak with thee, nor be with thee under one roof. May calamities fall upon thee and thy star be dimmed by clouds. . . ." The great ram's horn is sounded, and while its tones of doom fill the synagogue, one by one the candles are quenched until the congregation is left in total darkness. Such was the ceremony whereby Spinoza, greatest of modern philosophers, was cut adrift from the People of the Book, never again to the end of his life to have converse with his Jewish brethren. His father, a prosperous merchant, drove him from his home; his sister tried to cheat him out of a small inheritance; friends shunned him and pious ruffians attacked him. The young student became a wanderer, earning a meager livelihood.

As a boy Spinoza had no liking for business. He preferred to spend his time studying the learned books of the Jews. The elders prophesied that some day he would be a great leader of his people. Later Spinoza plunged into the mysteries of mathematics, physics and astronomy, and growing doubts made him question the beliefs of his people. He declared that the soul might merely be life itself, and that God must be too great to have revealed himself only to one people. For these heresies he was banished to what was tantamount to a living death—to complete social ostracism. In his lonesome room he formulated the philosophies which made hundreds flock to him as disciples. When his great work, "The Ethics," was completed, he dared not publish it, and left instructions that it be printed only after his death. It was not until then that the world became enriched by a work considered one of the outstanding achievements of the human intellect. He died while still young, a victim of consumption, and so poverty-stricken that his books had to be sold to pay the funeral expenses.

Israel ben Eliezer—Baal Shem Tob
(1700–1760)
FOUNDER OF HASIDISM

Israel ben Eliezer—Baal Shem Tob

IN 1648 there was a fierce Cossack uprising in Poland. More than half a million Jews were slaughtered without mercy in the ravages of that rebellion. For many years thereafter the surviving Jews suffered great hardships. By the middle of the eighteenth century several million Jews were dwelling in eastern Europe amidst unspeakable misery, poverty and ignorance. Forgotten became traditional Talmudic Judaism, and neglected and abandoned were the rabbis. Many, to bear their burden until "the coming of the Messiah," joined a cabalist sect which preached the mortification of the flesh and constant asceticism as the only services pleasing to God.

In these dark days there appeared among the Polish Jews one Israel ben Eliezer, later to be known as the Baal Shem Tob. He was born in Podolia and lived in humble circumstances. A legend says that his father, taken prisoner in a war, became a slave in an unknown land. Here, because of his great wit, he became confidant to the king. When he was one hundred years old he returned to his native country to beget a son, soon after whose birth both he and his wife, having accomplished their destiny, died. Israel, orphaned at four, was cared for by the townsfolk. He neglected his studies at school, and often ran away into the woods to lose himself in dreams. When he reached manhood he began to preach a new belief to the people. His message was that by simple prayer and the gift of the heart, mankind may influence God himself. He condemned those who worshiped God by fasting, abstinence and sadness, and instead preached joy and gladness in prayer. This new religion of tenderness, fervor and joy spread rapidly. "Hasidim"—the Pious—his followers called themselves. When they prayed they raised their voices high and swayed their bodies back and forth in ecstasy. Hasidism spread quickly all over eastern Europe. Thousands of weary Jews found solace in this spiritual ecstasy. A man of great humility and tenderness, the Baal Shem Tob became famed as a saint who could heal the physical and spiritual ills of man. To this day, Hasidism is still the religion of many Jews who firmly believe that the glory of God is only to be found where joy reigns.

Moses Mendelssohn

(1729–1786)

THE HUNCHBACK WHO ENLIGHTENED THE JEWS

Moses Mendelssohn

AT DESSAU, Germany, in the Ghetto home of a poor scribe of the Scrolls, Moses Mendelssohn was born. He spent his boyhood in the bareness of the Yeshiva, swaying backward and forward from morning to night chanting the Bible verses. At fifteen, his rabbi, to whom he was greatly devoted, was called to a congregation in Berlin. Moses put on his threadbare cloak, took his prayer-book and talith, and set out on foot to follow his rabbi. He was a strange-looking boy: short, clumsy, shy, hunchbacked, who stammered when he spoke. At the Berlin border a gruff Prussian sergeant refused to admit him. Poor, cold, frightened, and unable to speak clearly, he argued with the gatekeeper until he was admitted.

The years following were spent in wretched poverty. He lived in a garret, and often one loaf of bread had to suffice him for a week. He would divide the loaf into seven parts and each day he ate one of the sections. Alone in his garret he educated himself in the "liberal" subjects that were strictly forbidden by the elders. Early he came to the realization that his people were enslaved by their own restrictions. "Why could not one be a good Jew and at the same time a good European?" thought Moses. He decided to become the first modern Jew and to get in touch with his times and with the society in which he lived. He learned German and sought the company of learned Jews and Gentiles. The brilliant mind and personal charm of this misshapen Jew made him welcome everywhere. He was a man of great wit. When he met and fell in love with the beautiful daughter of a friend, the girl at first was frightened by his deformity. Once she asked him, "Do you believe then that marriages are made in heaven?" He answered, "Yes. When I was born my future wife was named, but it was said: 'Alas, she will have a dreadful humpback.' 'O God,' I said then, 'a deformed girl will be unhappy. Dear Lord, give me the humpback and let the maiden be born beautiful.'" Shortly afterward they were married. From this union sprang many brilliant children and grandchildren, of whom Felix Mendelssohn, the great composer, was one. Mendelssohn's life influenced Jews to seek enlightenment as citizens of a modern world.

Francis Salvador
(–1776)
INDIAN FIGHTER

Francis Salvador

FRANCIS SALVADOR was born in England of a wealthy family. In his boyhood he was sent to the finest English schools and given a liberal education. Wealthy, brilliant, and a fine figure of a man, he settled down to the peaceful pursuits of a London business man of high rank. At one blow, a great Lisbon earthquake and the collapse of the Dutch East India Company swept away his entire fortune. To retrieve his fortune he sailed off to America in 1773. He settled in the South, bought land, and within a year became the most prominent Jew living in South Carolina.

It was at this time that the colonists had begun to prepare for the War of Independence. Their ideals of liberty appealed to Salvador, and he became an intimate of the great Revolutionary leaders of the South. His southern neighbors held him in such high esteem that they elected him to the First and Second Provisional Congresses formed to draft a Bill of Rights, and he became a member of the South Carolina General Assembly. Meanwhile, bands of fierce Indians were raiding southern settlements and massacring all who fell in their power. Salvador recruited some troops and fought off the Indians. The red men feared him as the great, fearless, white Indian fighter. In 1776, British troops landed and attacked South Carolina, and incited the Cherokee Indians to attack and burn the white settlements. Salvador, learning of the plot, quickly gave the alarm, and recruiting a militia, he met the Indians and the Tory troops at Esseneka. In that bloody skirmish Salvador was shot off his horse and seized by the Indians and scalped. When the Indians were driven off, Salvador was found dying. A soldier bent over and spoke to him. Anxiously Salvador asked if the enemy had been beaten. When told that they were, he smiled, feebly shook the soldier's hand, whispered a farewell and a Godspeed to his men, and died.

Haym Salomon

(1740–1785)

AN AMERICAN PATRIOT

Haym Salomon

THE victory achieved by the colonies in the War for Independence was not won alone by the musket and fire of the patriots of 1776. There were other patriots, the men behind the war who financed the Revolution and made it possible for George Washington to lead his bedraggled army to victory and a nation to liberty. Haym Salomon was one of those heroes, and his story is one every American should know.

He was born in Lissa, Poland. He received an excellent education and mastered several languages. At thirty, a well-to-do merchant, he emigrated to the shores of liberal America and settled in New York. Here he established himself in business and prospered. A lover of liberty, he aligned himself with the colonists in their grievances against England. The British arrested him as a spy and charged him with receiving orders from General Washington and attempting to burn the British fleet in the harbor and destroy their storehouses. He was court-martialed and sentenced to death. But because of his wide knowledge of languages, a Hessian commander spared his life and appointed him purveyor for the officers. But Salomon continued to work secretly for the American cause in the enemy's camp. He assisted patriot prisoners held in New York to escape, and created dissension among the Hessian officers, prompting many of those mercenary soldiers to desert. For this he was arrested and again sentenced to be shot, but he escaped to Philadelphia. There he joined Robert Morris in the task of financing the Revolution. He raised large sums of money, poured his own fortune into the treasury, and collected other funds to buy guns and food for the soldiers. When the war was over, he was an impoverished man. He set up a brokerage business and soon recouped some of his losses. He continued to make huge loans to the new and struggling nation, and supported any public servant in want. This practice finally impoverished him. He remained a loyal Jew, donating large sums to charity. In the prime of his life he died, leaving his wife and children penniless. To Haym Salomon truly belongs the title of American Patriot.

Mayer Amschel Rothschild

(1743–1812)

FOUNDER OF THE HOUSE OF ROTHSCHILD

Mayer Amschel Rothschild

MAYER AMSCHEL ROTHSCHILD was born in the Ghetto of Frankfort-on-the-Main, son of a poor merchant. His father wanted to see his first-born grow up to be a learned man, and so sent him to the Yeshiva to study for the rabbinate. At eleven, Mayer was orphaned, and relatives in Hanover secured for him a post as messenger boy in a banking house. He remained there for eight years until he returned to Frankfort, where he found his two brothers established in a wretched little business as second-hand junk dealers. Understanding coins, trinkets and old jewelry, he joined his brothers, and the three became traders in works of art and curios. Mayer's vibrant energy, bright mind and personality made the business prosper and grow. Mothers with marriageable daughters took notice, the Ghetto matchmakers became active, and Mayer married pretty little Güttele Schnapper. Within sixteen years ten children were born to them, among whom were the five destined to become the famous sons of the House of Rothschild.

On the death of his brothers, Mayer inherited the business, but the humdrum life wearied him. No sooner were his sons confirmed than they commenced to take an active interest in their father's business. But Mayer discouraged them, for he yearned to be the father of scholars and hoped that his sons would not become dull tradesmen like himself. His financial genius brought him the appointment as agent and banker to one of the reigning princes of Germany. He transacted the business with profit both to himself and to the prince, thus laying the foundation for the fabulous Rothschild fortune. His sons, grown to manhood, settled in other countries and became powerful bankers. Old Mayer remained in his Ghetto home, advising and counseling his sons. He died without seeing them become the most powerful men in all Europe, wealthier than kings. His last words to his sons were, "Stand together always as one." Indomitable in their union, the House of Rothschild has written the most spectacular chapter in the financial and political history of Europe.

Isaac Franks

(1759–1822)

GEORGE WASHINGTON'S RIGHT-HAND MAN

Isaac Franks

ISAAC FRANKS was the son of one of the most distinguished American Jewish families of Colonial times. As a boy his imagination was fired by the growing movement for freedom from the yoke of English tyranny. When he was seventeen, the Revolutionary movement in the American colonies burst into open warfare. Young Isaac equipped himself with a rifle and boots, and enlisted in the Colonial Army of 1776.

He served under the command of George Washington and was appointed to the General's staff. He carried orders and dispatches on the battlefields and became recognized as Washington's right-hand man. In the historic Battle of Long Island, with the colonists' forces overwhelmed and fleeing in retreat from New York, Franks was captured by the British. He made a daring escape and rejoined Washington. The war over, Franks, now a colonel, returned to private life. Washington never forgot his comrade-in-arms, and Franks became one of Washington's closest friends. Among the patriots who fought to free the thirteen colonies in America from British rule, Franks' name stands high. For, in the words of Washington, "He was a soldier who served his country well and was concerned more with the welfare of his cause than the glory of his person."

Daniel Mendoza

(1763–1836)

KING OF THE ROPED ARENA

Daniel Mendoza

A HISTORY of boxing could not be written without telling the story of Daniel Mendoza. He was not only the first Jewish fighter of the prize ring, but also, after one hundred years, remains probably the greatest of Jewish fighters old or modern. Born in London, he was a handsome fellow and the possessor of a tremendous wallop. He entered the roped arena at the age of twenty-four, amazing the sports world with a new and never before seen boxing skill. Mendoza's name was on every Englishman's tongue. He became the founder of a distinct school of scientific boxing which marked a new period in the history of pugilism. No longer was prize fighting a sport of brute strength, but an exacting contest of skill. Mendoza became the most popular sporting hero of England, and in 1792 he was crowned heavyweight champion. They called him the Star of Israel, and popular ballads were composed celebrating his fighting deeds.

His fame spread far beyond his native land. He left his favorite London haunts and journeyed off on a triumphant tour, showing his boxing skill before huge crowds of sportsmen of all lands. He returned to England a celebrated hero. After a long and brilliant career in the ring he retired and, at different times, was an actor, merchant and letter-writer. Fourteen years later, an old man of fifty-seven, he re-entered the ring, but was beaten by younger opponents. Chagrined at his defeats, he retired permanently. He died in his seventy-third year, and to this very day England remembers the brilliant deeds of its great fistic warrior, while historians of the prize ring regard Mendoza as the first and one of the greatest exponents of scientific boxing.

Esther Manuel
(1784–1849)
WOMAN OF LOVE AND THUNDER

Esther Manuel

IN A LITTLE village of Prussia lived Esther Manuel, a young and beautiful Jewess. She fell in love with a Russian soldier and the two were married. With time, Esther became the mother of two children. Her life was peaceful and happy. But all too soon Europe woke to hear the fateful words, "Napoleon has escaped from Elba." Quickly the armies of Europe massed against the little Corsican. Esther's husband was called to the colors, and he marched off to fight with the Russian army. Esther's days of idyllic happiness were over. For weeks she brooded and pined for her husband. Then came a day when the news was brought to her that her husband had been lost in battle. She could not believe it. Some still, small voice in her heart told her that he was still alive. Obeying this compelling urge, she decided to search for him.

She cut off her beautiful long hair, dressed roughly in man's clothes, and enlisted in the Prussian army allied with the forces of the English Wellington to crush Napoleon. She fought bravely and with remarkable courage. Although twice wounded, she recovered, to win the Iron Cross for Valor and became a sergeant-major. At the campfires, the soldiers whispered of the deeds of this unknown Uhlan with features as delicate as those of a woman, but with the courage of a lion. For two years Esther lived the hard life of a Prussian soldier and never once betrayed her sex. Always she searched through the sea of marching faces and the thunder of tramping boots to find her husband. In 1814, in a battle under the walls of Paris, she found him, only to see him fall fatally wounded. Forgotten was her bravery, courage, and all thoughts of her disguise as she knelt beside him, raised his wounded head to her breast, and wept with unconsolable grief. Only then did her comrades realize that their brave sergeant-major was a woman. She was mustered out of the army and returned to her home with the military honors bestowed only upon the bravest of men. She was now thirty years old, and she remained in her native village with her two children. Throughout all Prussia for years thereafter, the great and the humble spoke of this brave woman who had performed such valiant deeds for love.

Sir Moses Montefiore

(1784–1885)

CHAMPION OF JEWISH RIGHTS

Sir Moses Montefiore

THE stories told of the deeds of Sir Moses Montefiore have become thrilling legends. Born in Italy, he lived most of his life in England. As a business man and financier he rose to wealth and power. A pious, God-fearing Jew, Montefiore became a great English patriot and adviser to Queen Victoria, who knighted him, an honor never till then bestowed on a Jew. The great triumphs of his life were in the cause of Jewish freedom. His greatest triumph was the historic Damascus affair.

In 1840 a number of Jews were arrested in Palestine, accused of killing a Franciscan monk in order to use his blood for ritual purposes. Darkness and gloom fell upon the Ghettos. Angry mobs raced through the streets, shrieking, "Kill the Jews!" Sir Moses hurried to Alexandria to the court of the powerful ruler and pleaded the cause of his unfortunate brethren. He proved the charges false and based on ignorance. The imprisoned Jews were released. Sir Moses then persuaded the Sultan of Turkey to issue the "Firman," which ordered his fanatical subjects to allow the Jews to practice their religion freely. The "Firman" is recognized as the Jewish Bill of Rights.

Wherever Jews were in distress, Sir Moses headed the struggle for their liberation. Hardship and danger meant nothing to him. Cruel persecution once broke out in Roumania, as crazed rioters plundered and murdered Jews. Sir Moses fearlessly ordered an open carriage and drove slowly through the streets shouting, "Plunder and kill if you choose, but I have come here in the name of Justice and Humanity. I trust in God. He will protect me!" Slowly the violence died down and the pogrom ceased. For sixty years he worked at the task of freeing Jews from oppression. He encouraged Jewish learning and spent his vast fortune for Jewish colonization in Palestine, being the first Jew permitted to buy land there. After a fruitful life of more than a century, he died honored by kings, princes and sultans.

Rebecca Gratz

(1781–1869)

HEROINE OF FICTION

Rebecca Gratz

WASHINGTON IRVING, the American author, visiting the famous novelist Sir Walter Scott, chanced to tell him the story of a lady he knew who was like a heroine of the Old Testament. She was beautiful of face, pure of heart, and loyal to her race—a Jewess who glorified all womanhood. Sir Walter was fascinated by the story. Two years later he sent to his American friend his new novel, "Ivanhoe." With it was a letter expressing the hope that the Rebecca of the book typified all that was noble in the real Rebecca. Thus did Rebecca Gratz inspire the imagination of a great author, and the nobility of her life confer literary immortality upon her.

Born in Philadelphia, daughter of a wealthy merchant, she was a girl of great beauty, charm and culture, and in womanhood a lady of wit and a hostess of social grace. Her salon was the gathering place of men of letters, financiers, statesmen, merchant-princes and fashionable society, at a time when Philadelphia was the social and political center of the United States. In her early twenties she fell in love with a Christian. A devout Jewess, she refused to marry him. Although many famous men thereafter sought her hand in marriage, she never forgot her first and only love and remained unmarried. She devoted her life to the poor and the unfortunate, and became a worker in charitable and religious causes. She founded orphanages and religious schools. Her charm and grace never left her. She died at a ripe old age, mourned as the foremost Jewess in the United States and one of the noblest women in the world. Her last words were, "I commit my spirit to the God who gave it, believing with a firm faith in the religion of my fathers. Hear O Israel, the Lord our God is one."

Uriah Phillips Levy
(1792–1862)
THE SEA FIGHTER

Uriah Phillips Levy

ALMOST from the moment he was born, Uriah Levy seemed destined for the sea. When only eleven, he ran away from his wealthy Philadelphia home and became a cabin boy. Before he was twenty, he was master and part owner of a schooner. His life was full of wild adventure. In 1812 his sailors mutinied, overpowered him, seized his ship, and left him to die on a deserted island. He was rescued, and after thrilling adventures found and captured the mutineers. He brought them back to the United States where they were convicted as murderers and thieves.

During the War of 1812 Levy became a commissioned sailing master of the United States Navy and helped capture several enemy vessels. His heroism and daring gained him promotion, and he was put in command of one of the captured ships. He roamed the high seas, attacking any ship flying the British flag, until his ship was captured, when he was taken to England as a prisoner of war. The American government remembered his bravery, and after he was freed, promoted him to the rank of lieutenant. The following forty years of his life in the navy were filled with bitter fighting against religious attack and prejudice on the part of jealous fellow officers. Quick tempered and proud, he resented their unjust slurs on his race, and fought a duel in which he killed his opponent. Six times he was court-martialed, dropped from rank, but finally reinstated and cleared of all guilt. Despite opposition, Levy gained promotion after promotion, rising to the grade of commodore, then the highest rank in the United States Navy—the first Jew to achieve such a distinction. As commodore, he fought against the ancient, barbarous practice of flogging on the high seas, with the result that a law was passed abolishing corporal punishment in the United States Navy.

Heinrich Heine
(1797–1856)
SINGER OF THE IMMORTALITY OF LOVE

Heinrich Heine

"O Tod! mit deiner Grabesstille, du,
Nur du kannst uns die beste Wollust geben!"

FROM the cradle to the grave, for Heine, the earth was a vale of tears. He was born in Düsseldorf, the son of a tradesman. At sixteen he was sent off to Frankfort to become a banker. But business wearied him, and he went to Berlin to live with a wealthy uncle. This pompous kinsman wanted young Heine to be a lawyer, and could not understand the strange boy who wasted his time writing poetry. Heine fell passionately in love with his uncle's beautiful daughter, Amelia. This vain lady treated him lightly, thus unconsciously earning the thanks of all lovers of beauty. For to still his aching heart, Heine wrote some of the tenderest love lyrics a poet ever penned. Tired of law, and suffering the pangs of unrequited love, he went off and lived alone in poverty, misery and illness. But he soon returned to his uncle's home, finished his studies, and became a lawyer. He wrote a book satirizing the stupidities of man and exposing the shams of modern civilization. It enraged official Germany and made Heine a marked man.

To escape arrest he went to England, then to Paris, but spies everywhere harassed him and made his life unbearable. During these months of physical and spiritual torment, he met and married an ignorant, poverty-stricken girl, Mathilde by name. During all the years she lived with him she hardly knew that her husband was a poet, nor heard of his growing fame. But to Heine's lonely and thwarted soul she brought the love and tenderness he craved.

Illness never deserted him, and Fate's last cruel blow was a paralysis that kept him suffering for years on his mattress-grave waiting for death. Jesting to the end, he said, "Jehovah, God of Justice, has paralyzed my lips so that I cannot even kiss." Thus ended life's weary journey for Heine. Only a handful of friends were near to weep for him—for Heine, singer of the immortality of love, poet whom the world will never forget.

Benjamin Disraeli
(1804–1881)
STATESMAN

Benjamin Disraeli

D ISRAELI once said, "Life is too short to be petty." His own life was stupendous. He was born in London, son of a wealthy Spanish Jew. Neglected by a father who was a successful novelist, and pampered by a doting mother, his older sister was his sole playmate. At school the boys treated the little Jew with hoots and jeers; only Benjamin's sturdy fists and indomitable pluck saved him from humiliation. His teachers disliked him, for his witty answers often embarrassed them. At fifteen he was dismissed from school for disobedience. Thereafter, eager for knowledge, he was for the most part self-educated. Even as a youth he dreamed of a great political career.

At seventeen he worked in a solicitor's office, but the life bored him. A friend encouraged him to write, and three years later Disraeli published his first novel. He became the talk of London, and wrote other successful novels. A dandy in dress, witty and gay, he was hailed as the social lion of London. He stood for Parliament, but was defeated. Persisting, on the fourth attempt he was elected. His first speech in the House of Commons was a sad failure. The members hooted the dandy with his hair in curls and rings on his fingers, forcing him to sit down, but Disraeli shouted, "Jest and laugh if you wish, but though I sit down now the time will come when you will all hear me!" Several years later, without political influence or Court favor, he became the leader of the House of Commons.

At heart he was a Jew ever proud of his descent. Once when attacked by an opponent as a member of an inferior race, he replied, "One half the world worships a Jew and the other half a Jewess." All England cheered his clever retort. At sixty-three he became Prime Minister of England. By brilliant diplomacy he purchased the Suez Canal, brought India under the Crown, and gave to Queen Victoria the title of Empress of India. Only after great persuasion did he accept a peerage and take the name of Lord Beaconsfield. Disraeli was an intriguing character—romantic, craving affection, loving art, wine and music. He spent his last days lonely and brooding, sitting in his study before a glowing fire, and murmuring, "Dreams, dreams, dreams."

Felix Mendelssohn

(1809–1847)

"A MIDSUMMER NIGHT'S DREAM"

Felix Mendelssohn

AT FOUR he was a pianist; at ten, a composer; at eighteen, a world celebrity; and at twenty-five, the most beloved musician of his time in all Europe. Such was Felix Mendelssohn, composer of the music of life, laughter and springtime.

He was born in Hamburg, the son of a rich banker. From childhood, surrounded with every luxury and comfort, Mendelssohn went through life with lively enthusiasm. Where other great composers knew poverty, misery, disappointment and neglect, Mendelssohn in all his gay life never faced an obstacle to fame.

His mother, who was a highly gifted and distinguished woman, gave him his first music lessons, and his cultured father did everything to foster his son's budding talent. At eighteen, handsome, witty and pampered idol of Europe's most brilliant society, Mendelssohn composed the famous "Midsummer Night's Dream" overture. From his precocious pen flowed other great works. Perhaps the greatest of his compositions was the oratorio of "Elijah." Kings, queens and other royalty bestowed great honors upon him, and young Mendelssohn won international fame. He lived a happy, carefree life, and his music reflected his joyous contentment.

Yet suddenly, Mendelssohn, who never knew sadness or a moment of worry or care, within the space of a few years lost his father and mother. A restlessness seized him. To drown his sorrow, he composed feverishly. One day, news was brought to him of the death of Fanny, his beloved sister. He became a victim of deliriums and possessed with the presentiment that death was hovering over him.

Before the year had passed, Mendelssohn, his wife and children beside him, passed peacefully away into immortality, to be remembered as a composer who left to the world a priceless heritage—beautiful songs of joy, life and laughter.

Judah Philip Benjamin

(1811–1884)

THE BRAIN OF THE CONFEDERACY

Judah Philip Benjamin

APRIL in 1865. The last shot of the Civil War had been fired. General Lee had surrendered, and the Confederate government had fallen. Through mud and muck the heroes and leaders of the South were fleeing to escape prison or exile. In the darkness of that fateful night rumbled a war-battered ambulance wagon. Hidden within it, disguised, was a fat little man, contentedly puffing a cigar and cheerfully reciting poetry. He was Judah Benjamin, the brain of the Confederacy, the same Judah Benjamin whom the Yankees would have been glad to capture and hang from the topmost branch of a tree.

This southern rebel was born on British soil. Poor and unknown he came to New Orleans, a young man, to seek fame and fortune. Starting as a law clerk, he became a lawyer. He entered politics and was elected senator from Louisiana. So brilliant was his political career that he was offered the post of Justice of the Supreme Court of the United States. But he refused the honor and threw in his lot with the South he loved so well. At the outbreak of the Civil War he was appointed Secretary of War and then Secretary of State of the Confederacy. He advised and counseled the leaders and generals of the South in their campaign against the North. When the guns ceased firing, Benjamin had to flee for his life. Reaching the coast he boarded a ship bound for England. There was a storm, the boat was wrecked, and Benjamin and a few other survivors drifted for days without food and water until rescued. After these and other turbulent and harrowing experiences he arrived in London.

The future looked dark and hopeless for this man, now fifty-four and penniless. After a bitter struggle, he once again established himself as an attorney and within fifteen years became one of the leading barristers of England. He became enormously rich, and the best homes in London were opened to him. But despite his new honors he was unhappy and longed to be back home in his beloved South. With this longing unfulfilled, he died—a man without a country. His monument in the South are the heroic legends which have been built around his deeds.

Karl Marx

(1818–1883)

PROPHET OF A NEW WORLD

Karl Marx

KARL MARX was the most hated, feared and slandered man of his age. He was born in Treves, Germany. For many generations all the male forbears both on his father's and mother's side had been rabbis. His father, however, was a lawyer. Marx was a brilliant child. At seventeen he entered the university. A year later he fell in love with a beautiful lady of noble birth and married her.

Marx was a poor breadwinner. He was always in debt to the grocer, the butcher and the landlord, and half his household goods were always at the pawnshop. Yet this man who could neither earn nor spend a penny wisely, elaborated the most profound of all economic theories. Marx was the prophet of a world system whereby everyone was to have a sufficient share in the world's goods. To establish this system became his mission in life.

A strange and lonely man was Karl Marx. He lacked comradely spirit. Both enemies and friends knew him for a fiery, violent and quarrelsome neurotic—proud, obstinate, pig-headed and hostile, yet a conscientious fighter with a tremendous capacity for self-sacrifice. But he could also be gentle and kind. Children loved him and knew him as "Daddy Marx," who always had a packet of candy for them.

At twenty-one he became a journalist. He edited radical newspapers and wrote numerous books and articles on social questions, for which he was expelled from Germany. The next thirty years he lived in London with his wife and three children in dreadful poverty.

When Marx was fifty he devoted himself completely to economic research. Nine years later he published the first volume of "Das Kapital," a profound analysis of political economy. The book was completely ignored, and Marx became sick, broken and disillusioned. In the midst of his great work, seated one afternoon in his study, he quietly dozed off and died in his sleep. Thousands of volumes have been written and bitter wars have been fought over the teachings of this prophet of a new economic order.

Abraham Schreiner

(1820–1900)

DISCOVERER OF PETROLEUM

Abraham Schreiner

IN BORYSLAW, Galicia, about the middle of the nineteenth century, lived Abraham Schreiner, a merchant. Needing a storage place for his business, he bought a little tract of land. When he came to build, he noticed upon the land a hollow from which exuded a greasy, tarry liquid. The peasant farmers of the neighborhood told him that this greasy earth possessed miraculous healing powers. The merchant's curiosity was aroused, and although he had no scientific training, he took some of the greasy soil and began to experiment with it. Forming a ball of the stuff, he inserted a wick and lighted it. Fascinated, he stood watching while the mass burned with a strange, red flame. Continuing with his crude experiments, he extracted the liquid from the mass and tested it in an old-fashioned vegetable-oil lamp. This experiment led directly to the construction of the first petroleum lamp in the world.

Forgotten now was his business and his plans to build a storage house upon the land. Instead, he dug a well and set up pumps. Trying to distill the substance, he filled an iron pot with it and placed it on a lighted stove. The pot exploded and he was badly burned. No sooner had he recovered than he took instructions in distilling from the local apothecary. This resulted in his producing petroleum which was sold in bottles to the public. The use of this refined oil spread quickly. Schreiner took all the money he could raise, bought pumps and sunk wells to procure oil in larger quantities. He built a factory, but the building caught fire. He rebuilt it, and again the factory burned down, leaving him penniless. Old and too poor to start all over again, a broken man, he opened a little dram shop to earn his livelihood. There he spent his remaining days in poverty, selling liquor to the very peasants who were earning their livelihoods in the industry which he had started.

Rachel

(1821–1858)

TRAGIC MUSE

Rachel

BORN in a humble wayside cottage in a Swiss village, Rachel rose from the gutter to hear the applause of the world. Her father was a wandering peddler, and her mother a dealer in second-hand clothes. At ten, dressed in rags, Rachel and her little sister sang in cheap cafés for the coins thrown at them. When she returned to the hovel that was her home, abuse and kicks were largely her rewards. Knowing neither love, kindness nor laughter, she grew into a dreamy girl—small, frail, undernourished, ugly, often mocked at as the "half-starved monkey." At thirteen she made her first public appearance in a theater.

Her rise was phenomenal, and before long she was acting in Paris, and all France was at her feet. Her fame spread to other countries. She made whirlwind tours to foreign lands. Royalty and commoners alike fell under the magic of her unparalleled genius. She had an amazing gift for learning quickly, and soon the great actress was also a woman of extraordinary wit and charm. Famous men and women crowded her salon and sought her friendship.

A woman of many passions, many virtues and many faults, the theater was her very life. On one occasion, well past midnight, she was rehearsing a play. All the other actors had left. Her audience in that darkened theater consisted of the author of the play and the stage doorman. Never had she acted so well. When she was praised for projecting herself with so much realism into the tragic rôle of the dying heroine of the play, Rachel dropped a tear and said, "I am weeping not for her but for myself, for I too will die young and no trace will be left of my talent, and nothing at all of her who once was Rachel." It was not long after this that, still young, she died of consumption. But the fame of her genius remains imperishable.

Joseph Israels
(1824–1911)
PAINTER OF THE SOUL

Joseph Israels

SON of a poor Holland merchant, the boyhood of Joseph Israels was not a very happy one. Often he went without sufficient food and clothing. His father wanted him to be a rabbi and sent him at an early age to study the Talmud. But the boy was possessed of a restless and creative urge, and his mother, seeing how anxious little Joseph was to learn drawing, scraped up some money for private lessons. The town teacher had no praise for him. He thought the boy's method of drawing too slovenly and often said that he had no talent whatever.

At sixteen Israels left his native town and went to Amsterdam. For five years he studied painting and lived in dire poverty. The first picture he painted for public exhibition used up such a large quantity of a particularly expensive white pigment, that it took him four years to repay the dealer for the cost of the materials. When he was thirty, after a severe illness, he went to live in a poor fishing village on the North Sea. He loved the simple folk and became engrossed with the beauty and tranquillity of their humble lives. For fifty years he devoted himself to painting pictures of hard-working peasants and fishermen. He was hailed as the painter of the soul. The Dutch government recognized him as the painter-interpreter of its people and bought many of his paintings to hang in the national galleries.

Eighty years old, Israels turned his fertile brush to Jewish subjects. His paintings expressed the deep emotion, pain, joy, fortitude and solemn beauty of his own race. At his death Israels was recognized as one of the greatest Dutch painters of the nineteenth century. His canvasses hang in all the important art galleries of the world.

Baron Maurice de Hirsch

(1831–1896)

PHILANTHROPIST

Baron Maurice de Hirsch

NO MAN in the entire history of philanthropy has donated more money and benefited more people by his far-flung munificence than Baron de Hirsch. During his lifetime he gave away to charity more than one hundred million dollars. He was born in Munich, the son of a rich nobleman. At manhood he entered the business world and increased the fortune he had inherited by many successful railroad and financial ventures. He was considered the greatest industrialist in all Europe.

Living in luxury, he knew little of the suffering of his Jewish brethren. On a visit to the Orient he was shocked to see the wretched condition of the Jews dwelling there. His heart was touched, and he contributed a large sum of money to relieve their distress. When he heard stories of Jews in other lands suffering from poverty and persecution, he began to interest himself in their welfare. Here he contributed a million francs to a school system, and there he donated two million dollars to a home for unfortunates.

He was especially aroused by the plight of the Russian Jews. He offered the Czar fifty million francs to improve the condition of the Jews in Russia. When the government wanted to tie up his gift with unfair restrictions, he decided to help Russian Jews to emigrate from their hopeless surroundings. He financed Jewish colonies in Argentina, Canada and the United States. To encourage Jewish immigration to these colonies he formed an association and endowed it with ten million dollars. To it he bequeathed most of his vast fortune. In New York he founded trade and industrial schools. His charities were not confined to his own people, but he gave lavishly to numerous non-sectarian institutions. When he died he was mourned by millions of every creed and country.

Siegfried Marcus

(1831–1898)

GRANDFATHER OF THE AUTOMOBILE

Siegfried Marcus

EARLY in the nineteenth century in Vienna, the seventeen-year-old Siegfried Marcus graduated from technical school as one of its ablest engineers. He found employment with a large engineering firm and performed such brilliant work that within ten years he achieved financial independence. He retired and established a laboratory of his own in which to devote all his time to inventing. Soon all Vienna heard of this remarkable engineer in whose busy little shop many useful inventions were developed. He invented the first electrical fuse suitable for underwater explosions, a seismograph, and devices for the regulation and measurement of heat and for the discharge of deep-sea mines by electricity. But the young inventor was possessed of a far greater dream—to invent a self-propelling carriage.

In 1864 he built his first horseless buggy, but it was not much of a success. The neighbors laughed at its clumsy progress, and little boys threw stones at it. Another eleven years of patient plodding, then one day the people of Vienna stopped to look in wonderment as they saw a horseless carriage driven through the streets by a man who sat inside it and steered. He had at last invented his benzine-fuelled engine which fundamentally is the same as today's high-speed motor car. Marcus was an impractical business man and neglected to patent his invention until several years had passed. Meanwhile, in other lands inventors were tinkering in their laboratories with the horseless carriage, and soon they too perfected a self-propelling vehicle. Thus Marcus never gained the fame and fortune that might have been his. He is hardly ever mentioned in the history of the automobile, yet his brain-child was the basis for the millions of automobiles driven today on every highway of the world.

Ivan Stanislavovich Bloch

(1836–1901)

FIERY ADVOCATE OF UNIVERSAL PEACE

Ivan Stanislavovich Bloch

WHILE a young man Ivan Bloch earned his living as a peddler hawking his wares on the streets of Warsaw. As soon as he had acquired enough money, he threw away his pack and went to Berlin to study. Returning to his native land, he gained a high reputation as an economist and sociologist, and became Poland's most influential banker and railroad builder. He married a talented woman and his home became the intellectual center of Poland.

A lover of peace and a practical business man, Bloch realized that war was a menace to the economic welfare of nations. He saw the need for ending war and substituting for it some rational, civilized way of settling international disputes. He became a fiery advocate of universal peace, and wrote six volumes on the folly of war and the urgent necessity for abolishing it from the civilized world. This monumental work, translated into almost every European language, startled emperors, kings, rulers, statesmen, and thinking men and women all over the world. His denunciation of war, his eloquent pleading, his scientific consideration of the problem, stirred government circles. As a result of Bloch's persistent agitation, measures were taken which resulted in the formation of the Peace Conference of 1899 at The Hague, then in the establishment of The Hague Tribunal, now known as the World Court of the League of Nations.

Bloch died in the midst of his great work, firmly believing that one day the nations would rise and abolish the ugly specter of war from the earth. His memory will always be cherished as a man who lived, worked and died so that there might be peace on earth.

Georges Bizet

(1838–1875)

COMPOSER OF "CARMEN"

Georges Bizet

WHO has not heard the opera "Carmen"? It has been sung in every language known to civilized man. Carmen, the madcap Gypsy girl, meets Don José, the soldier. He falls under her spell, deserts his regiment and his sweetheart, and runs off with her to join a Gypsy band of smugglers. Soon the fickle Carmen falls in love with a new hero, Escamillo, the handsome toreador. On the day of the bullfight, Don José stabs the faithless Carmen, and as the gay crowds leave the arena, the murderer denounces himself, flinging himself across her dead body with a cry of love and despair. This is briefly the story of the great lyric opera composed by Georges Bizet.

Bizet was born to music. His father was a Paris singing teacher, and his mother a pianist. At the age of four, instead of playing games, the child would stand listening at his father's studio door. When he was eight he surprised his parents by singing perfectly the most difficult lessons which he had heard his father teach his students. He was taken to a conservatory, but the professor protested that the child was too young to be admitted. "Strike any chord on the piano and I will name it," said little Georges. The professor did so and was amazed to hear the boy identify the most difficult chords and explain their different functions. He was admitted to the classes and quickly distinguished himself by winning many prizes over students far older than himself.

In 1875 the Opéra Comique presented Bizet's opera "Carmen." The audience received it coldly. Bizet was depressed, convinced that the opera was a failure. Three months later, at the age of thirty-seven, he died of a heart affliction, never to know the popularity which his opera would achieve. If no other music of his survives, Carmen alone will insure the fame of Georges Bizet.

Emin Pasha

(1840–1892)

EMPIRE BUILDER

Emin Pasha

I N THE last half of the nineteenth century there appeared in Constantinople—that polyglot city of the East—a young, penniless German
doctor of medicine. His name was Eduard Schnitzer. He was an unheroic
figure of a man—nearsighted, bespectacled, wearing a fez and observing
Mohammedan rites. Emin Pasha he called himself. Nothing much was known
of the little doctor except that he was skilled in chess, fluent in many languages, and with a wide scientific knowledge. He spent his time roaming the
countryside studying bird and plant life, or else he sat for long hours at the
piano playing the music of Chopin and Mendelssohn. For five months he
drifted about the Turkish post, making friends with Egyptians and Arabs
until one day he went steaming up the Nile as a government medical officer.
Two years passed, and then the news came from the Sudan that His Excel-
lency, the new Governor of Equatoria, was none other than Emin Pasha.

No one who had known him could believe that the peaceful, timid little
doctor could rule that vast, savage African state. But he could and he did.
In the heart of darkest Africa he controlled a huge empire, and for ten years
ruled supreme. He broke up the nefarious slave trade, explored the sources
of the Nile, and journeyed into the unexplored jungles of Africa to secure
valuable collections of botanical and zoölogical specimens. There was a native
uprising, and all news of Emin Pasha was lost to the outside world for several
years. Stanley, the great explorer, organized a rescue party and after years of
terrible hardship succeeded in finding Emin alive, but ill and half-blind.
Recovered in health, he refused all honors and undertook another exploration
into the interior. Walking away from camp one day, he was attacked by two
Arabs and assassinated. For months his death was not known until a European
officer found some books and diaries and learned that they were the records of
the famous Emin Pasha. To this very day his place of burial remains a mystery. But wherever adventure beckons there hovers the spirit of the mysterious
Emin Pasha.

Luigi Luzzatti
(1841–1927)
GRAND OLD MAN OF ITALY

Luigi Luzzatti

BORN the son of one of the leading Jewish families in Venice, Luigi Luzzatti was given a liberal education. At nine, a healthy, robust boy who played well at all sports, he was taught Italian literature, philosophy and natural science. He could not understand why the other boys mocked him for being a Jew, and, hot-tempered, often fought them. Once he threw a boy twice his size into a canal, but when he saw his tormentor could not swim, jumped in after him, pulled him out, and begged his forgiveness.

Because of his mother's wish, he entered the university to study law, but he had little taste for it, and after he graduated, never practiced the profession. Economics interested him most, and the improvement of the lot of the Italian working masses. He started a mutual aid society for underpaid gondoliers and had to flee Venice to escape arrest on a charge of treason. He became a teacher and preached his ideas of mutual aid, people's banks and popular credit. Before he was thirty he entered politics. When Italy was on the verge of bankruptcy, Luigi was appointed Minister of the Treasury, a difficult and thankless job. He restored Italy's finances and saved his country from imminent financial collapse. This made him renowned throughout Europe as Italy's greatest economist. Luzzatti was the first to establish people's savings banks and originated a law for compulsory accident insurance. These measures are now in force in all civilized countries. At sixty-nine he became Prime Minister of Italy. Hating oppression and persecution, he fought to destroy it in all countries. Often he served as peacemaker between foreign powers and negotiated treaties which gave a new economic life to Italy. An old man, he retired to his home in Rome where daily there flowed a procession of princes of the blood, foreign diplomats, cabinet ministers, rabbis, bankers, merchants and humble men of all faiths to seek his advice and support for their projects. Even Mussolini, the Italian dictator, often sought Luzzatti's approval on important measures. He died mourned by all as the Grand Old Man of Italy.

Nathan Strauss

(1848–1931)

PRINCE OF THE GENEROUS HEART

Nathan Strauss

"WHAT you give after death is lead; what you give in sickness is silver; what you give in life is gold," says the Talmud. The gifts of Nathan Strauss were gold; he was a generous philanthropist all his long life. Born in Bavaria, he came to America at the age of six. His early childhood was spent in the South. His father was prosperous, but during the Civil War the Strauss fortune was swept away. The father brought his family to New York and started a business in pottery and glassware, while Nathan, now in early manhood, was sent to business college. He later joined his father's firm and proved an extraordinary merchant. Under his management the business prospered.

One day he visited the slums of the city. The emaciated children of the poor aroused his pity. He made the appalling discovery that many of these babies were dying because of the impure milk fed to them. At that time the Frenchman Pasteur had discovered a method of destroying the disease germs in milk. Strauss went to Europe to investigate the Pasteur method. He returned to America, and, in the face of attacks from purveyors of milk and even from physicians, he opened depots in the public parks where Pasteurized milk was sold to the poor at half price. The results were amazing. Other cities followed suit and also established milk depots. Strauss gave up his business affiliations and devoted himself entirely to philanthropic works. He founded the first tuberculosis preventarium for children, established lodging houses for the homeless, and food stations for the hungry. A devout Jew, he longed to see the homeland of his people. When he arrived in Palestine and saw the wretched conditions there, he spent vast sums of money in the building of a water system to supply pure water, and from Europe he brought great eye specialists to set up clinics for the treatment and cure of the natives ravaged by blindness. He built schools for the education of the children, soup kitchens for the poor, and a factory so that hundreds could be employed and earn a livelihood. Until the day of his death, he worked selflessly for all mankind. He will be remembered by this and future generations as the merchant-prince of the generous purse and the open heart.

Otto Lilienthal

(1848–1896)

THE BIRD MAN

Otto Lilienthal

A
S A BOY Otto Lilienthal was fascinated by the flight of birds. Little was
known at that time of the mechanics of flying, of the airship or the
aëroplane. The son of an engineer, Otto was sent early to a technical school.
After graduation he became a busy engineer, traveling about his native Germany on important business missions. But he never forgot the kites and model
airships which he had built in his boyhood days, and the hours he had spent
enviously watching the flight of birds.

By the time he had passed his fortieth birthday, several mechanical devices
which he had invented made him wealthy. He retired from business affairs
and devoted all his time to flying experiments. He built a machine that had
two wings like those of a bird, with a tail at the rear for balancing. Launching
himself into the air by running down the slope of a hill, much as modern
gliders do today, he soared off the ground with a vigorous thrust of his legs.
The people of the countryside were amazed and frightened by the queer antics
of this strange bird man.

For twenty-five years he had experimented and made over two thousand
flights. One cold and stormy day, he went to the top of a hill to perform a trial
flight. His brother tried to dissuade him from flying in such bad weather.
Fearless as ever, Otto laughed at danger and set off in a glide. He was flying
successfully when suddenly a gust of wind struck his machine, crashed it to
the ground, and Lilienthal was killed.

Aviation since that day has made great strides. But wherever motors roar
in the blue, and man-made birds fly in the air, Otto Lilienthal is remembered
as the fearless pioneer of the aëroplane.

Albert Michelson

(1852–1931)

HE MEASURED THE SPEED OF LIGHT

Albert Michelson

WHEN Albert Michelson was seventeen years old, a boy in San Francisco, his ambition was to study at the United States Naval Academy. To gain an appointment he traveled across the continent to plead his case personally before Ulysses S. Grant, then President of the United States. The President liked the young lad and admired his determination, and he was appointed to Annapolis. At school he devoted so much of his time to science that the superintendent of the Academy remarked, "If you'd give less attention to those scientific things, and more to your naval gunnery, there might come a time when you will know enough to be of some use to your country." Upon his graduation, Michelson embarked on a career that made him one of the foremost of world scientists.

He was born in Prussia and came to America as a young boy. Upon graduation from Annapolis he was detailed to teach physics and chemistry at the Academy. There, along the sea wall at Annapolis, he first began to conduct his light-measuring experiments. After years of epochal work, he computed that light travels 186,213 miles per second, a figure which scientists of the world have accepted. This was one of the great scientific contributions of the age. It was his researches in light that paved the way for one of the most startling of modern conceptions, Einstein's Theory of Relativity. No scientist possessed a greater passion or ability for accurate and detailed work than Michelson. He devised an instrument known as an interferometer with which scientists were able to measure for the first time the diameter of stars. At seventy-seven, internationally famous and the recipient of the Nobel Prize, he undertook a new series of experiments to determine more exactly the speed of light. When urged to rest his frail body he replied, "When my last experiment is completed maybe I'll take life easy and begin to think about retiring." Soon after he died, to be mourned as one of the great scientists of modern times.

Paul Ehrlich
August von Wassermann
(Ehrlich—1854–1917)
(Wassermann—1866–1925)
HEROES OF THE LABORATORY

Paul Ehrlich
August von Wassermann

THE men who labor in the secret recesses of the experimental labora- tory to discover the unknown for the benefit of all mankind are the true heroes. Two such men were Paul Ehrlich and August von Wassermann. Ehr- lich, born in Silesia, was the most celebrated scientist and original scientific thinker of his time. He had little enthusiasm for medicine, but studied it because his mother insisted that her son become a doctor. At school he was a mediocre student who had to force himself to memorize the names of the bones and the muscles of the bodies he dissected. But his interest flared up, and by the time he was twenty-five he had startled the medical world with his work on the diseases of the blood. He originated the "side-chain" theory, which proved that the living protoplasmic molecules making up the human body consist of an unchanging center or nucleus. For ten years he worked alone to discover a cure for syphilis. He prepared six hundred and five compounds and remedies. They all failed. On the six hundred and sixth experiment he was successful in discovering salvarsan, and the world became enriched by one of the most important discoveries ever made in medicine. The cure is now generally known as "606." He received the Nobel Prize and was decorated by kings and emperors. Ill and old, he died while working in his laboratory.

Wassermann, too, was interested in the domain of immunity, but without Ehrlich's "side-chain" theory he would not have been able to discover the "Wassermann test." He was born in Germany. As a doctor he was exceedingly clever, at the same time a brilliant speaker who shone at all great medical gatherings. Keenly alert in his work he always added something fresh and new to the discoveries of other scientists. In 1906 he discovered the so called Wassermann reaction in the diagnosis of syphilis. He attained world fame, and his name became a household word. The Wassermann test is now em- ployed in every pathological laboratory in the civilized world.

Louis Brandeis
(1856–1941)
FRIEND OF JUSTICE AND OF MAN

Louis Brandeis

NO JEW in America reflects greater glory upon Israel than Louis Brandeis, and no American has served America with greater devotion. He was born in Louisville, Kentucky, in humble surroundings, the son of an immigrant. At eighteen he entered law school, and when he graduated, poor and unknown, he opened a law office in Boston. Within eight years he became the leading barrister of that city. On his wedding day he confided to his bride that he was wealthy enough to retire and devote the remainder of his life to public work.

To the surprise of the wealthy social set in which he moved, Brandeis began to interest himself in labor organizations and to champion the underdog whenever and wherever human rights were in jeopardy. His interest in Jewish matters began at this time. Invited to serve as arbitrator in a New York garment strike, he learned for the first time of Jewish problems. He became a Zionist, and a leader in the fight to reawaken the Jewish spirit and safeguard Jewish rights. In 1916 President Wilson appointed him to the United States Supreme Court. Industry, finance and powerful interests all over the country assailed the President for naming Brandeis to the highest court in the land. To all critics President Wilson replied, "He is a friend of justice." After a few years on the bench he was hailed by the once prejudiced press as America's greatest jurist.

Louis Brandeis retired from the bench of the United States Supreme Court in 1939, loved, honored and esteemed as "A friend of justice and of man."

Sigmund Freud
(1856–1939)
EXPLORER OF THE HUMAN MIND

Sigmund Freud

SIGMUND FREUD was born in Freiberg, Moravia. As a child his chief delight was in playing with wooden soldiers. He named each toy soldier after a famous general, but the rôle of the greatest warrior of them all he reserved for himself, and dreamed that some day, as a great conqueror, he would march on Rome. Grown to manhood he studied medicine, but had little enthusiasm for it. He was shy, sensitive, possessed of a deep feeling of inferiority. His university classes were torture to him. Fellow students mocked him as a Jew. To escape their jibes he plunged deeply into his studies. He would prove to the world that a Jew can be as great and even greater than those about him.

An unknown doctor at thirty, he groped deep into the unconscious and subconscious thoughts of man, his dreams and phantasies, and tried to reach the wellsprings of human conduct and behavior. He learned of a case of hysteria cured by hypnosis. After considerable research along this line, he rejected the factor of hypnosis and developed the "free association" idea, and from this the entire system of psycho-analysis. His theories and conclusions were bitterly attacked and reviled. Scorned and scoffed at, he persisted, gaining adherents, fighting the virulent attacks of doctors and psychologists. His fame has become world-wide. His cures have amazed the medical world, and his name is known all over the civilized globe. Psycho-analysis has become an accepted method for the treatment of neuroses and the basis of a new school of philosophic thought.

Adolph Ochs

(1858–1935)

ALL THE NEWS THAT'S FIT TO PRINT

Adolph Ochs

H E WAS born in the South to a father of excellent education and a cultured and brilliant mother. Their influence upon him was immense and lasting. His father, a pious, scholarly idealist, was not much of a provider for his wife and children. Adolph, the oldest, was forced to seek work at the age of eleven. His first job was office boy on the local newspaper. His chief duty was to clean the editor's desk. Soon he was promoted to the position of delivery boy at a weekly salary of one dollar and fifty cents. Then he became a "printer's devil." He learned the newspaper business in an amusing way. Daily he worked until dark. Young and timid, he was afraid to walk home alone, for he had to pass a cemetery. Therefore he would spend hours doing odd jobs about the composing room until the foreman, who lived in his neighborhood, was ready to go home.

When the "Chattanooga Times" suffered a financial collapse, young Adolph, a reporter of twenty, borrowed some money and bought the bankrupt newspaper. With a private fortune of thirty-seven dollars and fifty cents he became a publisher. As he could not afford a staff, his entire family collaborated in getting out the paper, while Adolph was everything from editor to errand boy. The paper prospered and became one of the leading newspapers of the South. For eighteen years, Ochs was at the helm while leaders of politics, industry and finance sought his advice and support on matters of national importance.

At thirty-eight, when "The New York Times" fell upon evil days and no one seemed willing to tackle the job of reviving the bankrupt newspaper, Ochs bought it. It seemed a perilous and hopeless task. But within a few years, Ochs made the "Times" one of the most influential newspapers in America, and he became one of the most important newspaper publishers in the world. "The New York Times," probably the greatest newspaper in the world, is Adolph Ochs's monument.

Alfred Dreyfus

(1859–1935)

DEVIL'S ISLAND COULD NOT CRUSH HIS SPIRIT

Alfred Dreyfus

MARTYR or traitor? Dreyfus was the principal figure in one of the most passionately debated political controversies in French history. Born of well-to-do parents, Dreyfus pictured himself from boyhood as a dashing soldier leading his men into battle for the glory and honor of his native France. At eighteen he enrolled in the National Military Academy. His progress was rapid, and he was made a captain on the military staff of the War Department—the first Jew to be given such a post. Brother officers envied and hated him. In 1894 he was arrested and accused of revealing military secrets to Germany. He was court-martialed, publicly degraded, and condemned to life imprisonment on Devil's Island. As they broke his sword and ripped the insignia from his uniform, Dreyfus cried, "I am innocent. Some day all will know the truth. Long live France! Long live the Army!" But vengeful mobs outside the garrison gates shouted, "Judas! Traitor!" For five years, imprisoned in the desolate, tropical, fever-ridden Devil's Island, Dreyfus suffered untold tortures. His case was debated all over the world and many duels were fought because of it. France stood on trial before the world. The distinguished novelist Emile Zola wrote a passionate defense of Dreyfus, attacking the trumped up evidence of the conspirators, and beginning each paragraph with the ringing words: "J'accuse!" The cry swept round the world. Forgeries came to light. The diabolical plot to convict an innocent man was exposed. A new trial was ordered, but again the prejudiced military court found him guilty. This time, so outraged was the nation and the world, that the President of France had to pardon him, but Dreyfus refused to accept anything less than a complete exoneration. For seven years he followed the trail of the conspirators until he was completely vindicated and his honor restored. Commissioned a major, in the World War he again proved himself a loyal soldier, and was elected to the Legion of Honor. He retired from the Army and spent the rest of his life quietly in a little house in Paris. In death as in life he remained a symbol of Liberty and Justice.

Rufus Daniel Isaacs
(1860–1935)

Rufus Daniel Isaacs

A SCORE of years before the close of the nineteenth century a coal ship steamed into an Indian port. On deck stood a boy—a seaman serving before the mast. He had left a luxurious home in London and had run off to sea to escape the monotony of the schoolroom and to answer the call of adventure. As the ship nosed its way into the harbor, the restless boy, burning with eagerness, caught his first glimpse of that mysterious land. Almost half a century later, amidst pomp and ceremony, a British warship steamed into India. On its deck stood the same boy, now a gray-haired man. He was returning to India not as a grimy sailor but as the honored Marquis of Reading, Viceroy of India. His mission was to govern the lives of more than three hundred million people in the name of the English Crown. Therein lies the life story of Rufus Isaacs, an English Jew who rose to an eminence in the British Empire unknown since the days of the glamorous Disraeli.

Rufus Isaacs was the son of a prosperous fruit merchant. As a boy he abandoned his schoolbooks to seek the excitement of a sailor's life. But his father brought him home and sent him to finish his studies, hoping that the boy would, in time, become a successful merchant. Rufus wanted to study for the bar, but his father disapproved, and so the boy decided to sail for America. His mother stopped him as he walked up the gangplank of the ship, and persuaded him to return on the promise that he would be permitted to study law. Within eleven years he became the recognized leader of the English bar. He entered politics and, after holding several important posts, was appointed Lord Chief Justice of England, the first Jew ever thus honored. As a reward for his service to the Empire he was knighted. In the World War he proved himself a great statesman and diplomat, and came to America as special ambassador to the United States. No Englishman of this century has played a more active and significant rôle in British affairs than Reading—a true son of the Empire.

Theodore Herzl

(1860–1904)

"IF I FORGET THEE, O JERUSALEM"

Theodore Herzl

BORN in Budapest, Theodore Herzl, at twenty, was a celebrated playwright and journalist in Vienna. He was in Paris, as correspondent for his paper, when the Dreyfus case burst upon the world. Seeing the hatred shown to his people even by a civilized country like France, he became alarmed over the welfare of the Jews scattered among the nations of the world. From that day, his goal was the emancipation of the Jews as a people.

He wrote his book called "The Jewish State" to express the need for a Jewish homeland. At thirty-six, leader of the Zionist organization, Herzl was hailed by millions of Jews as their savior. For eight years he devoted his talents as a writer, orator and politician to secure for his people an internationally recognized homeland. He pleaded his cause before pope, sultan, king, kaiser and czar, and sought the aid of the world's richest financiers. He failed everywhere, but the massacres of Jews throughout Europe drove him with increased fervor to find a national home for his people.

Palestine was then a locked door, and Herzl was willing to accept Uganda, a British East African possession, which England wished to bestow on the Jewish people. The masses of Jews refused to follow Herzl in this project and forsake their hopes for a home in the land of their fathers. Even his friends deserted him. Despondent, weary and ill, the father of political Zionism died in the prime of his life. But Zionism lives on, and Herzl's name is implanted forever in the hearts of Jews the world over.

Arthur Schnitzler

(1862–1931)

MASTER OF TWILIGHT MOODS

Arthur Schnitzler

BORN in Vienna, Schnitzler was the son of a famous Viennese throat specialist. To his father's office celebrated theatrical figures of the time came for treatment. They stimulated young Arthur to the romance and excitement of the half world of illusion. In the boy of five, there was awakened a desire to write plays, and at that tender age he wrote his first five-act tragedy.

As the years passed, his father frowned on a literary career and insisted his son follow the medical profession. He graduated from the University of Vienna and entered upon a medical career. For a time he saw active hospital service and enjoyed an extensive practice as a doctor for thirty years.

But doctoring could not still the urge to write. From his pen flowed a stream of witty verses and sketches, and Vienna came to know of the satirical artist who so brilliantly probed the frailties of human nature.

A year after his father's death, Schnitzler discarded the scalpel for the pen and began in earnest his career as a writer. A member of a respectable upper middle-class family and possessed of an extreme sense of moral responsibility, he had never experienced the frivolities of youth and love. In his mind there arose a subconscious admiration for the gay people who flitted about loving and dying in that magic world of spring, color and adventure. His creative work became largely an expression of his melancholy yearning for such a life. He unmasked his characters of their suppressed desires and hidden soul secrets. Schnitzler indeed was the foremost disciple of Freudism in the drama.

He became internationally famous as a delicate craftsman who portrayed twilight moods and the strangeness and loneliness of the life of men and women. He shrank before the specter of old age and feared loneliness, yet most of his life he lived in semi-seclusion. On October 21, 1931, in the midst of writing his play "The Call of Life," he suffered a fatal heart attack.

Schnitzler has taken his rank among the masters of literature. Of him it has been truly said, "Wilde fortified with Ibsen—Vienna crossed with Paris."

Israel Zangwill

(1864–1926)

THE JEWISH DICKENS

Israel Zangwill

NOVELIST, playwright, poet, interpreter of the glory of Israel—this was Israel Zangwill. In his youth he knew poverty and suffering, but rose to write his name high among the topmost in the scroll of the great. Born in the Ghetto of London, he spent his boyhood in the humble, orthodox home of his father. He was eager for knowledge, and despite many obstacles, studied avidly. He was brilliant. At the schools of Whitechapel, at the university, everywhere he took honors.

The tragedies and comedies of the Ghetto—the ceaseless surge of Jewish life that flowed before his understanding eyes—impressed themselves deeply in his heart. As a young man he became a journalist, but he could never hold a job long. His scintillating wit always seemed to offend the pompous shams of someone in power. While still in his early twenties he wrote "Children of the Ghetto." It lifted him to fame and success. He wrote other books and turned his fertile pen to the stage, becoming one of England's greatest playwrights.

He was passionate in his Jewishness and a bitter critic of Jewish faults. An ardent Zionist, Zangwill was an untiring worker in the cause. He influenced countless thousands of Jews throughout the world, and is reverenced by them as the spokesman and interpreter of their joys and sufferings, their pleasures and their pains.

Carl Laemmle
(1867–1939)
LITTLE GIANT

Carl Laemmle

ONE of the greatest and most spectacular moving-picture pioneers who blazed the trail to Hollywood, Carl Laemmle was born in Laupheim, Germany. At thirteen he was apprenticed as an errand boy. He was so small for his age that when the proprietor of the little town store saw him, he protested against taking Carl. Later, he drudged away for years as a bookkeeper. His desire to go to America was strong, and on his seventeenth birthday his father presented him with the gift of a steerage ticket to the United States. He arrived in New York with a battered valise and fifty dollars. His first job, at four dollars a week, was washing bottles and sweeping floors. After a time, he drifted out West. At the age of forty, he was manager of a clothing store.

One day he took his life's savings of twenty-five hundred dollars and went to Chicago to open a five-and-ten-cent store. He saw a gaping crowd paying to enter a hall and see the marvelous new invention—motion pictures. On an impulse, he invested his entire capital, hired an empty little store, and opened a nickelodeon—a five-cent picture house. His business soared to prosperity, and Laemmle decided to organize his own moving-picture company, only to discover that the industry was controlled by a powerful group who would not allow an independent producer to enter the field. Undaunted, he filmed his pictures in secret lest strong-arm men of the trust smash his cameras. He waged so bitter a fight that he forced the government to dissolve the trust. He built Universal City, and was the first producer to film serious dramatic pictures. Among his discoveries were an unknown girl and a poor waiter in a restaurant, whom he sent on to fame as Mary Pickford and Rudolph Valentino.

Lillian Wald

(1867–1940)

THE ANGEL OF HENRY STREET

Lillian Wald

IN NEW YORK CITY, on a crowded thoroughfare of the East Side known as Henry Street, stands a house which presidents of the United States, prime ministers, and famous men and women from every nation have come to visit. It is the home of Lillian Wald. In 1893 she had left her college books and laboratory in Ohio and come to New York to work as a nurse. On a cold March morning, a poor, frightened little girl knocked at the door of the East Side home where Miss Wald lived, and whimpered in broken English, "My mamma she die." The nurse followed the child to a wretched, poverty-stricken home where a woman lay dying. The young Lillian, from a cheerful home of plenty, was shocked by this sight of human suffering. She was horrified to realize that society in America's greatest city could so neglect its poor. To help these unfortunates became her life's work.

With little money, but great courage, she rented a house. There, with the aid of another nurse, a home was opened where the helpless and unemployed who could not avail themselves of hospitals, could come for aid in time of sickness and need. Thus was founded the Henry Street Settlement, the most famous institution of its kind in the world. Lillian Wald found her way into the homes and hearts of the people of the neighborhood. They trusted and worshiped this angel of mercy. She fought with politicians and lawmakers for housing reforms, child protection, and the elimination of social evils. She gathered other nurses about her and they ministered to the poor and sick and instructed mothers in cleanliness and hygiene. Today the Visiting Nurse Service of the Henry Street Settlement reaches the entire city and has become a model for communities the world over. More than 100,000 patients are cared for every year. Through the procession of almost half a century of peace, war, prosperity and depression, Lillian Wald lived on Henry Street fighting against poverty, ignorance and disease. To her settlement have come fathers, mothers, boys and girls to play, to learn, and to become useful citizens of their country.

Karl Landsteiner

(1868–1943)

THE BLOOD DETECTIVE

Karl Landsteiner

YEARLY the lives of thousands of people the world over are snatched from death by a timely blood transfusion. Yet, not so many years ago, saving a human being's ebbing life by injecting into the body the blood of another person was a haphazard and dangerous experiment. Often, the patient died because the blood of the two bodies did not match. Today, blood matching is a precise science, and blood transfusion a successful and simple everyday hospital routine. All this has been made possible by the labors of Dr. Karl Landsteiner.

Landsteiner was born in Vienna, the son of a doctor. Following the family tradition he studied medicine. He worked as a pathologist and began to do research work with blood. He discovered that different individuals have different blood characteristics and began to classify blood groups and make tests to observe the reactions to transfusions. This work became the starting point for a series of advances in medical knowledge which thirty years later was to bring world fame to Landsteiner.

Carefully and accurately Landsteiner noted his observations, and after many experiments, he finally suggested the use of the blood group for medical purposes. He conducted experiments, too, in immunology and susceptibility. He was able to produce in a monkey the dread disease of infantile paralysis. This started other investigators on a series of experiments for the cure of this scourge. All that is now known of the cause and cure of this disease is directly due to Landsteiner's original monkey experiments. Landsteiner received the Nobel Prize and was hailed as one of the great scientists of his time. His experiments on blood transfusion mark one of the great advances in the history of medicine.

Bernard Mannes Baruch
(1869–   )
INTIMATE OF PRESIDENTS

Bernard Mannes Baruch

ONCE a little boy born in South Carolina came to New York. His father took him for a walk through the streets of the big city. The little boy was awed by everything he saw. When he stopped and gazed in wonder at a towering skyscraper, his father took his hand and said, "Come along, my son. If you're good and work hard you'll own much bigger buildings than that some day." That little boy was Bernard Baruch, the multimillionaire financier.

He is the bugaboo and mystery man of Wall Street, the financial heart of the world. Years ago he made his appearance in Wall Street and in daring market manipulations piled up a vast fortune. During the World War President Wilson appointed him head of the War Industries Board, a job that made him virtually economic dictator of the country. There were plenty of critics to cry out against the appointment of a Wall Street operator to this important post, but Baruch proved so efficient at his job that he turned his bitterest critics into staunch admirers. Wise and trustworthy, he has been the intimate adviser to three Presidents of the United States. Today he is one of President Roosevelt's closest counselors. Long before the great Wall Street panic of 1929, Baruch urged the most powerful bankers of the country to form a pool so that the market could be sustained. He offered to contribute six million dollars for the purpose, but the proposal was rejected.

Among his chief interests are agriculture and the raising of the status of the American farmer from his state of impoverishment to financial comfort. Tall, suave, handsome, Baruch flits in and out of the White House and for many years has played an important rôle behind the scenes in government affairs. A statesman without portfolio, he is one of the most important figures in the United States today.

Sir Herbert Samuel

(1870–   )

FIRST HIGH COMMISSIONER OF PALESTINE

Sir Herbert Samuel

ENGLAND has had more glamorous statesmen, and the destinies of the far-flung British Empire have been piloted by more dashing figures, but none has ever served his country with greater skill, wisdom, or higher purpose than Sir Herbert Samuel. His career has been neither exciting nor thrilling, but there has never been a single failure. One of the most powerful and influential statesmen in the affairs of the British Empire, his distinguished reputation was not made overnight by a single, daring stroke of statesmanship. It grew slowly and painstakingly, until today Sir Herbert is one of the greatest living statesmen. He is a quiet, unobtrusive, placid man. In the midst of a crisis, when the fate of the Empire is in the balance and while other ministers of state may become frightened or confused, he remains clear-eyed, calm and unruffled.

He was born in Liverpool, the son of an orthodox father. To this day, despite his international fame, he has remained the orthodox son of his father. While still a student at Oxford University, he became interested in politics, aligned himself with the liberal movement, and presented himself as a candidate for Parliament. After three defeats he was elected. Since then Sir Herbert has served his country in practically every important state post in the British government. He was knighted by King George V.

With the placing of Palestine under a British Mandate in 1921, he was chosen the first High Commissioner of Palestine. Depopulated, impoverished, and a boiling pot of politics and racial hates, this little country presented one of the most complex problems on the face of the globe. Yet during five years of his rule, waste lands were reclaimed, forests were planted, waters harnessed for electrical power, ports, roads and railways built, and a foundation for a system of public utilities was laid, comparable to any in Europe and America.

Sir Herbert Samuel was the guiding genius in these endeavors. He it was who laid the pattern for Palestine's future greatness.

Chaim Weizmann

(1873–1952)

BUILDER OF THE JEWISH HOMELAND

Chaim Weizmann

I T WAS 1915, the second year of the great World War. England and her Allies were facing a serious crisis. Because of the enemy's submarine blockade on the high seas, a vital ingredient for their explosives could not be shipped through to the Allies. Victory or defeat hung in the balance. Then, at the moment of gravest crisis, startling news came of a great discovery in a London laboratory. A Jewish chemist had developed a new formula for obtaining alcohol from wood, a material absolutely essential for the production of explosives. The chemist was summoned to the palace. Lloyd George, Prime Minister of England, faced the scientific genius and said, "The Empire and the Allies feel a debt of deep gratitude to you. What can we do for you in the way of any honor?" Whereupon the chemist replied, "I seek no great things for myself. All I care for is the opportunity to do something for my people." Two years later the British government kept its promise to the Jewish chemist and issued the famous Balfour Declaration. This declared to the world that England would co-operate in the reconstruction of Palestine as a Jewish homeland.

Thus the dream in the mind of a boy born in an obscure Russian village became a reality. For even as a little boy, Weizmann was troubled by the fate and destiny of his people. But boyish dreams gave way to chemistry studies in Germany and Switzerland, and at twenty-four Weizmann received his degree. Drawn into a circle of ardent Zionists, he became the leader of a group of young men planning to raise funds for the purchase of Palestine from the Turks. But this ambitious plan was abandoned, and he found himself in England lecturing on chemistry at a university. He became a British subject. At the issuance of the historic Balfour Declaration, he gave up his career as a chemist and plunged himself into the work of making Palestine the Jewish homeland. With the outbreak of World War II, Weizmann returned to his laboratory and the manufacture of synthetic rubber but as soon as hostilities ended, he again took up his crusade for a nation of Israel. In May 1948, his life-long task was accomplished and Israel was reborn. Chaim Weizmann became its first President.

Max Reinhardt

(1873–1943)

"ALL THE WORLD'S A STAGE"

Max Reinhardt

ONE morning in 1890, Max Reinhardt, then a young lad of seventeen, hurried to the railway station in the town of Baden. Although he had been born in Baden, he felt little sorrow as he boarded the train, for he was on his way to gay Vienna, to embark on a stage career. No longer would he toil in the musty old banking house where he had been apprenticed for years. Instead, he would become a great and famous actor. When he arrived at the theater where he had been promised a job, he discovered that all the actors paid the manager for the privilege of acting on the stage. Since he had no money, he sadly left Vienna and went to Salzburg. There fortune was a little kinder, and Reinhardt found an engagement portraying elderly character parts. For several years he trouped with touring companies until he found himself in Berlin.

While playing at a Berlin theater, Reinhardt and some friends, to amuse themselves, started a series of cabaret shows after the evening performances. From a few intimate friends as spectators, the novelty of the show reached the ears of the jaded Berlin theater-goers. They flocked to the cabaret. Soon, so great became his success that Reinhardt took over the theater. From that intimate beginning, he began to produce other plays. Gathering around him an incomparable company of actors and artists, he presented the finest plays of the world's greatest playwrights. Reinhardt created a new intimacy between the stage and the audience which led to the establishment of the little theater movement throughout the world. His dramas, miracle plays, pageants, his unusual scenic arrangements, color and lighting became the talk of all Europe. He went to Salzburg and staged the now famous Play Festival. Reinhardt became famous and rich. Other countries invited him to stage his productions in the important capitals of the world. In Hollywood he worked his magic on the motion-picture screen.

Stephen Samuel Wise

(1874–1949)

THE VOICE FOR HUMAN RIGHTS

Stephen Samuel Wise

STEPHEN S. WISE, world-renowned rabbi, was one of the most dramatic figures in the pulpit during this century. He devoted himself not only to religion but also lent his voice to every human cause. He came to America from Budapest when he was one year old, the son of an orthodox rabbi. At the early age of nineteen, he was ordained a rabbi and went West. For seven years his life was fierce and stormy. From his pulpit he discussed public questions, attacked crooked politicians, and told his congregation the truth about the social evils of their city. The young rabbi became known.

At this time, one of New York's largest and wealthiest congregations was in search of a rabbi for its pulpit. The young Rabbi Wise was invited, but with the reservation that he consent to the censoring of his sermons if they proved distasteful to the congregation. The rabbi refused the job with a bang. Loudly, through the press of the nation, he denounced the "muzzled pulpit." Wise became a national figure. Resolving to go to New York and preach his liberal Judaism, he founded the Free Synagogue. Championing a thousand causes, not only Jews but Gentiles also came to hear him. He was a valiant fighter for woman suffrage in the early days of that historic struggle and was among the first to champion Zionism in America. His forcefulness and eloquence aroused wide interest. He was attacked and praised. He spoke his mind even when it alienated his supporters. He had planned to build a new million-dollar synagogue. The wealthy and influential members of his congregation promised to help him raise the funds. At that time the steel workers were on strike. Wise attacked many of his congregation who were large shareholders in the steel industry. They withdrew their support and his plans for a new synagogue collapsed. Still fighting wherever corruption, oppression and injustice reared their heads; his pulpit became a tremendous national force and a power for social reform.

Herbert H. Lehman

(1878–   )

CHIEF OF THE EMPIRE STATE

Herbert H. Lehman

ON A DECEMBER day in 1929, Franklin Roosevelt, Governor of New York State, was away from the Executive Mansion. Acting for him as Chief Executive was Herbert H. Lehman, the little-known, extremely modest, almost shy business man who forsook a successful banking career to become the Lieutenant Governor of the state. As he sat at his desk, the telephone rang and startling news came of a rebellion that had broken out among the convicts at Auburn Prison. Twelve convicts had seized the warden and a group of prison guards and had killed the principal keeper. Freedom for themselves or death for the warden and guards was their demand. Herbert Lehman did not hesitate. His reply was, "There will be no compromise!"

There was a pitched battle. All the desperate prisoners were either killed or captured. The warden and the guards were saved. Thus did Herbert Lehman emerge from obscurity to stand forth as a public official of spirit, force and power—a man who could not be bluffed or intimidated when critical issues were at stake.

When Franklin Roosevelt became President of the United States, Herbert Lehman was elected Governor of the Empire State.

He was born in New York City, the son of a wealthy banker. Upon graduating from college, he joined his father's investment bank. At night he worked at the Henry Street Settlement on the East Side. He took little interest in politics. But in 1913 he was appointed a member of the commission to revise the banking laws of the state. So conspicuous was his ability that soon he was drafted to run for public office. He became a labor conciliator, and his tact and judgment averted many serious strikes and made the workers trust him as a friend. As Governor, he vigorously fought sweatshops, protected the young and defended the aged. He championed humanitarian laws and an adequate social security program. He became a powerful national figure whom President Roosevelt called "That splendid right hand of mine." In 1950 he was elected to the United States Senate from the State of New York.

Leon Blum

(1872–1950)

FRANCE'S MASTER OF DESTINY

Leon Blum

FRANCE, in 1936, faced a crisis. The Third Republic was at the crossroads. Fascism or Communism—these were the grave issues. If France was to take the middle of the road, only one man could lead it. That man was Leon Blum. Elected Premier in 1936, he was the first Jew to head a French government.

Leon Blum was born in Alsace, the son of a wealthy silk merchant of Paris. His childhood was sheltered. At school he was a brilliant scholar, attending the exclusive *École Normale Supérieure*. Upon graduation he went in for a literary career and earned high repute in French literary circles. He was aloof from politics and indifferent to the problems and struggles of his country.

The Dreyfuss affair was the turning point in his life. Leon Blum passionately entered into the debates that were shaking all France. He became a lawyer and entered the political arena as a Socialist. He was elected to the Chamber of Deputies. His eloquence, sharp logic, and fearless leadership in important national issues won for him command over the Socialists in the Chamber—the dominant political group of the day.

Enemies villified him and mocked him as "the millionaire Socialist." He was the victim of brutal and vicious attacks that threatened his life, but he continued to fight for social and economic reforms. In 1938 he was again elected Premier. He strongly opposed "appeasement" and the Munich pact. He was arrested by the Germans in 1940 after the fall of France and was later sent to a prison in Austria from which he was released by the Allies in May, 1945. In January 1946 he was appointed Ambassador Extraordinary.

Leon Trotsky

(1879–1940)

FORSAKEN NAPOLEON

Leon Trotsky

LEON TROTSKY is either loved or despised. At the height of his power he was the supreme war lord over the greatest army in the world—ten million fighting men. Born in a tiny mud-thatched farmhouse, his father was a prosperous Russian peasant farmer, Bronstein by name. As a little boy, Leon was taught reading and writing so that he could keep his father's account books. At seventeen, a student in Odessa, he fell in with a revolutionary group and organized a union of workers. For this he was arrested and sent to Siberia. By means of a forged passport he escaped to England. The passport he signed "Trotsky," the name of his jailer, and the one he has since retained. In London he met Lenin, a refugee plotting the Russian revolution. After the Russo-Japanese War, Trotsky went back to his native Russia to join the ill-fated Moscow uprising. The rebellion was crushed, and again Trotsky was sent to Siberia, this time for life. In a wild and daring dash on foot and by reindeer across the frozen wastes, he again escaped. For a while he lived in America and edited a small Russian newspaper in New York.

At the news of the fall of the Czar, Trotsky returned to Russia, where he joined Lenin in seizing control of the government. As Minister of War, he built a powerful army from a rabble of untrained, ignorant peasants, and by his personal bravery swayed them to unimagined sacrifices. A man of fierce action, he was a ringing advocate for peace. He tried to turn the vast Red Army into a labor army to reconstruct Russia. Never a diplomat, impatient, outspoken, he fell out with the Soviet leaders. After Lenin's death, he was deposed from high office and exiled from Russia. He sought refuge in Constantinople, France, and Norway; and finally found a haven in Mexico where he lived until he was murdered in 1940. He is the author of many pamphlets and histories of the Russian Revolution.

Jacob Epstein

(1880–   )

STORM CENTER OF SCULPTURE

Jacob Epstein

THE significant career of Jacob Epstein, a New York Jew, began when, after studying sculpture in Paris, he arrived in London a poor, unknown artist. For days he tramped the streets until he rented a stable and opened it as his studio workshop. He worked in this studio for years, giving sculpture a new interpretation. But no one knew and no one cared. Then, by a stroke of luck, he was commissioned to carve the figures decorating a new British medical building. At the unveiling, newspapers, artists and the public attacked Epstein's work. It was strange and different and seemed to violate all the canons of art. The attack became almost a nation-wide riot, and thus Jacob Epstein made his bow to the world of art.

He has remained a storm center. His enemies revile his work as blasphemous, sensational and mad, while his supporters hail him as the creator of a new epoch in art. The man himself has become an enigma.

Now famous, he lives in a large house in London. He never speaks to defend himself; he is too busy creating his sculptures, many of which have found their place in the most famous galleries of the world. His work achieves extraordinary effects of light. Critics who have tried to place his work, have found him an artist who belongs to no period at all. Condemned or revered, he marches along perpetuating his dreams and his individuality in enduring images. Only posterity will tell if Jacob Epstein is to take his place as one of the great sculptors of the world.

Casimir Funk

(1884–   )

ISOLATOR OF THE VITAMIN

Casimir Funk

FOR centuries the scourge of beri-beri, rickets, scurvy and similar diseases had caused untold suffering. Scientists all over the world conducted experiment after experiment to perfect a preventive and cure for these maladies. At last, in 1912, came the report of the discovery of the influence of the anti-beri-beri vitamin in milk, and in 1914 followed the isolation of the vitamin itself.

The discoverer was the Polish-born Casimir Funk, a research chemist in the Lister Institute of London. He had experimented for years with particular foods and their effect on disease, to determine the special constituents which acted as cures and preventives. An outstanding series of experiments with sick pigeons resulted in curing them of nervous disorders by confining their diet to husks of rice.

Now the understanding of vitamins, the part they play in human diet, and how essential the knowledge of them is to the welfare of the human body, is a vital weapon in mankind's fight for health. Outside his laboratory, Casimir Funk is little known to the world. Yet who can truly estimate how many millions of lives his genius has been instrumental in saving since his epoch-making discovery.

David Sarnoff

(1891–   )

S O S

David Sarnoff

ONE day in 1912, a twenty-one-year-old wireless operator sat at his land post tinkering with his instruments. It had been a long and weary day and he was tired. Suddenly, he sat up tense and eager. The telegraph keys were clicking out an exciting message. It was an S O S. Somewhere on the high seas, a ship was in distress. Intently he listened to catch every signal coming over the air waves. When he learned the name of the ship he sprang into action to spread the alarm. The *Titanic* was sinking! The *Titanic!* That huge, beautiful floating palace that was carrying thousands of people across the ocean. The first radio operator in America to pick up the distress signals, he worked feverishly, and within a few hours a whole nation was aghast at the horror of that fearful sea tragedy. For seventeen hours the young radio operator sat at his post, receiving and sending to a waiting world the full reports of the frightful sea disaster in which more than a thousand went to a watery grave. The whole nation came to know of this diligent and heroic radio operator, and David Sarnoff became famous.

Sarnoff was born in Russia, and in his boyhood was intended for the rabbinate. At the age of nine he came to America, and at fifteen he was orphaned. To help support his younger brothers and sisters, he worked as a newsboy. In spare moments he schooled himself. He found a job as messenger boy with the Marconi Wireless Telegraph Company. Radio fascinated him and often he spent twelve to eighteen hours a day learning its technique. Sarnoff became a radio operator working on land and sea. Thus began a climb to wealth and fame that is unparalleled in the entire world of radio. At thirty-one he became head of the Radio Corporation of America, the most powerful radio business organization in the world. He has been honored by American and foreign governments for his contributions to commercial radio development. Today, he is one of America's leading executives and one of the most powerful figures in the world of radio.

George Gershwin

(1898–1937)

FROM TIN PAN ALLEY TO CARNEGIE HALL

George Gershwin

GEORGE GERSHWIN was the youngest son of a family that lived on New York's East Side. It was by pure accident that George became a musician and composer. There was never any hint of musical talent in the Gershwin family tree. One day his mother bought a second-hand piano, more for a decoration than as a hope of having it played. But what good is a piano unless someone plays it? So, although little George seemed fascinated by the mysterious keyboard, his elder brother was chosen to become the piano player. But he hated the drudgery of piano lessons and showed little liking for music, and George crowded him out and usurped his place as the musician of the Gershwin family—a happy turn of events for the musical history of America. Very quickly George mastered all the knowledge that his twenty-five-cent-a-lesson teacher could impart. Often he would sit at the piano and improvise strange and fantastic tunes. A great love for music developed and grew stronger in him. There is a story that once, after hearing a famous violinist play, Gershwin stood for three hours in a driving rain for the chance to accost him and murmur a few words of bashful admiration.

At seventeen, George left school to devote himself to a career of music. For a while he plugged songs in Tin Pan Alley, the Broadway section where America's popular songs are born. His father was not so sure that his Georgie would amount to much. At about this time America was being inundated by the flood of jazz music, the newest craze. The music was loud, crude and savage. With little technical knowledge, Gershwin wrote a composition which he called "Rhapsody in Blue." It thrilled the nation and established Gershwin as a major American composer. Following that success, he composed numerous songs for Broadway musical productions and a nation hummed and whistled his songs. By the time he was thirty he was internationally famous. Today, he is considered one of the greatest of modern composers. His music is rich with exquisite color and rhythm. In concert halls, in theaters, and in millions of homes, there are constantly played the melodies of George Gershwin, who came from the sidewalks of New York to write the songs of a nation.

Jasha Heifetz
(1901–   )
KNIGHT OF THE BOW

Albert Einstein

ALBERT EINSTEIN was born at Ulm-on-the-Danube. As a child, he was mentally awkward, learning to talk slowly and with such difficulty that his mother feared she had given birth to an imbecilic child. He was a strange boy, shy, timid and dreamy. He loved solitude, and while other little boys played at games, little Albert would hide or walk in his father's garden, humming little songs which he had composed. One day he was shown a compass. The swinging needle awakened a great wonderment in him. At school he was an indifferent pupil, but showed surprising genius at mathematics. After graduation from the university he became a clerk in the Swiss Patent Office. At night he studied science and mathematics. He was then twenty-six years old.

At that time, the greatest scientists of the world were engaged in a series of experiments to determine how fast the earth travels through space. In every experiment they tried, their observations of the behavior of light indicated that the earth must be stationary. This was a baffling problem, for the reality of the earth's motion through space was proved by natural phenomena, yet the experiments of the scientists denied it. Einstein solved this mystery. His intricate mathematical calculations showed that the true explanation must take into account the position of the observer. He showed that nature is in continuous motion and that all motion is relative, and that one could never ascertain the motion of the earth except in relation to some other body in the heavens. To the accepted dimensions of length, width and height, he added another—time.

Einstein's theory burst like a bombshell on the scientific world and gripped the imagination of mankind. It withstood every challenge and test and forced science to adopt a new and revolutionary concept of the universe. Hailed as the Newton of the twentieth century, Einstein's name will remain immortal as the map maker of a universe.